Is Emotion Dead?

Learn How To Build Emotional Intelligence

By: Terence A. Williams

TABLE OF CONTENTS

Publishers Notes 3

Dedication 4

Chapter 1- What Is Emotional Intelligence and Why Is It Important? 5

Chapter 2- How To Improve Your Emotional Intelligence 9

Chapter 3- How to Apply Emotional Intelligence Techniques to the Workplace 13

Chapter 4- How Does Emotional Intelligence Help Leadership Skills 16

Chapter 5- What Are the Key Points about Emotional Intelligence? 19

Chapter 6- Developing Emotional Intelligence to Improve Your Mindset 23

Chapter 7- Understanding Emotional Intelligence and Communication Styles 26

Chapter 8- 7 Real Life Benefits of High Emotional Intelligence 31

About The Author 35

Publishers Notes

Disclaimer

This publication is intended to provide helpful and informative material. It is not intended to diagnose, treat, cure, or prevent any health problem or condition, nor is intended to replace the advice of a physician. No action should be taken solely on the contents of this book. Always consult your physician or qualified health-care professional on any matters regarding your health and before adopting any suggestions in this book or drawing inferences from it.

The author and publisher specifically disclaim all responsibility for any liability, loss or risk, personal or otherwise, which is incurred as a consequence, directly or indirectly, from the use or application of any contents of this book.

Any and all product names referenced within this book are the trademarks of their respective owners. None of these owners have sponsored, authorized, endorsed, or approved this book.

Always read all information provided by the manufacturers' product labels before using their products. The author and publisher are not responsible for claims made by manufacturers.

© **2013**

Manufactured in the United States of America

Dedication

This book is dedicated to my uncle Timothy, who encouraged me and my siblings to always feed our minds with information. True power can only be gained from improving ones knowledge.

Chapter 1- What Is Emotional Intelligence and Why Is It Important?

Emotional intelligence has become a hot topic over the past several years. Today's workforce has noticed that through emotional intelligence it becomes easier to operate successful companies. Since businesses are the people and workers who run them, it only makes sense that those people's emotions will play a large role in how the businesses are operated. For some experts, a person's emotional intelligence quotient is of much greater importance than his or her traditional IQ.

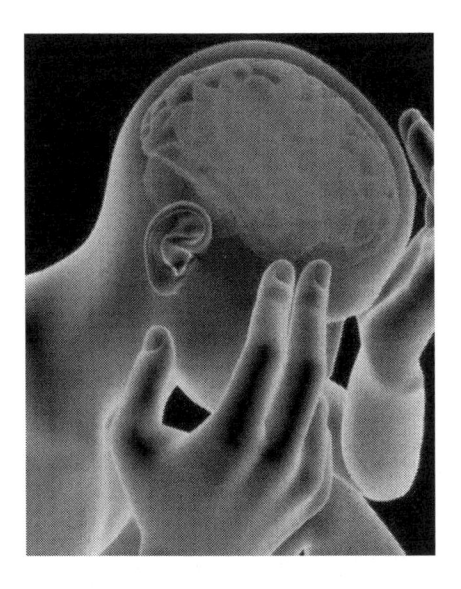

It is interesting to note how the world's view of emotional intelligence has changed over the years. During the 1930's, it was referred to as social intelligence. As time went on, during the mid-20th century, it becomes deemed as emotional strength. Nowadays, however, we refer to it as emotional intelligence. No matter the name it is referred to as it is very important. Through emotional intelligence, it becomes possible for humans to:

Self-Management: Manage and control both emotions and reactions to current circumstances

Self-Awareness: Identify and understand emotions

Motivation: Use emotions as motivation so that appropriate actions can be taken to follow through on commitments

Social Skills: Create relationships, carry out effective conflict resolution techniques and be a good leader

Empathy: Identify the feelings of others, and use those feelings so that it becomes easier to relate with other people

Understanding the Importance of Emotional Intelligence

Mental Well-Being: It is through emotional intelligence that a person acquires his or her outlook on life. With strong emotional intelligence, it becomes possible for a person to alleviate high levels of anxiety as well as avoid depression. There is a direct correlation between a high level of emotional intelligence and a good attitude.

Success: Because this type of intelligence helps a person to have strong internal motivation, with high levels of it, a person will have increased self-confidence as well as improve his or her ability to stay on track when it comes to achieving a certain goal. Emotional intelligence also helps a person to create strong networks among friends, family and coworkers, helping him or her to be more resilient during trying times.

Physical Health: Through strong emotional intelligence, it becomes more likely that a person will have good health. The reasoning behind this is because a person will continually think about the choices that he or she is making, followed then by making choices that improve his or her overall health. Those with low levels of emotional intelligence tend to be people who don't think ahead to what their actions and behaviors will bring about, meaning they oftentimes make choices with no thought to how it will affect their health.

Relationships: When a person is able to identify and understand his or her emotions, it becomes easier to communicate the emotions. In doing this, it is possible to build strong relationships. When two people who care about each other have high levels of emotional intelligence, they will understand both the needs and wants of each other, followed then by helping one another fulfill them.

Conflict Resolution: In order for a conflict to be effectively resolved, it is of the utmost importance for a person to discern the feelings of all parties involved. With emotional intelligence, it becomes possible to discern the feelings, and many times, it even becomes possible to avoid a conflict before it begins. All in all, this type of intelligence helps a person to perceive what it is that the person wants, making it easier to resolve the conflict.

Leadership: Those with high levels of emotional intelligence oftentimes make great leaders. They are able to understand the ins-and-outs of what it takes to motivate other people. They are able to relate to other people in a positive manner. Furthermore, they are able to build strong relationships with the people who they are around. These leaders can identify the needs of those around them, as well as develop solutions to meet such needs. Most importantly, through emotional intelligence, the leaders are able to identify diversity within teams, followed then by using these diversities to bring the team together so that it will function to its highest level of possible productivity.

When thinking about emotional intelligence, it is important to keep in mind that there is no exact definition used to describe it. Since no two human beings are exactly alike, emotional intelligence from one person to the next will somewhat differ. For those who are looking to advance in their career, taking part in workshops that help develop emotional intelligence can be very advantageous. For all others, it is still of equal importance to understand and carry out emotional intelligence as this helps one to enjoy life to the fullest degree possible.

Chapter 2 - How To Improve Your Emotional Intelligence

Even though the talk about emotional intelligence has grown in popularity over the past several years, there are still many people who have no idea what the concept is all about. When trying to understand this form of intelligence, it is important to keep in mind that it has a great deal to do with one's ability to perceive and control their emotions- both in his or herself as well as in other people- and use the perceived information in an appropriate manner. Having emotional intelligence will translate into a person being able to regulate emotions, all the while recognizing the emotions of others and being empathetic with them; this will help a person to be successful in life as well as to develop strong relationships with friends and loved ones.

So, the real question is, how does one go about developing a high level of emotional intelligence? For some, it comes completely naturally. For others, however, it is something that must be developed. Thankfully, there are several tips that can be followed to help with the development emotional intelligence.

Tip 1: Thinking about Feelings

Before dismissing feelings, it is important for a person to think them through. Sometimes, there is a very good reason for feeling a certain way. It is also important to keep in mind that even the healthiest of emotions are those that rise and fall. Overall, when it comes to managing emotions, it is pertinent not to cut them off before they have the chance to fully develop. Also, by thinking about feelings, a person will be more likely to sort through the negative and positive ones; thus, providing him or her with the opportunity to overcome the ones that are harmful.

Tip 2: Listening to the Body

Oftentimes, people will experience the feeling of having a "knot" in their stomach; this is a sure sign that too much stress is being endured. When it comes to being emotionally intelligent, this means a person won't ignore his or her body. By listening to the sensations that the body produces, this enables a person to process such feelings using the powers of reason.

Tip 3: Identifying Connections

Being emotionally intelligent involves being able to recognize certain feelings and connecting them with other times in one's life that similar feelings were felt. In being able to do this, a person can determine whether or not current feelings are linked with a current situation, or rather to some circumstance that occurred in the past.

Tip 4: Talk to Someone Else

Sometimes, the best judge of a person's feelings is another person. When doing this, it is extremely important to turn to a person who can be trusted. The answers that such a person is able to provide will many times be both interesting and enlightening.

Tip 5: Connecting Feelings with Thoughts

When something strikes a person out of the ordinary, it is useful to identify the reasoning behind it. In fact, by connecting feelings with thoughts, it becomes possible to view all angles of a situation, which enables a person to make better decisions.

Tip 6: Pay Attention to Dreams

By paying attention to dreams, a person can be more aware of his or her feelings. Even though some dreams can be incredibly bizarre, almost always there is some aspect of a dream that is derived from real-life wants and needs. By identifying these needs and meeting them, a person can then live a happier life.

Tip 7: Journaling

Keeping a journal is an excellent way to improve one's own level of emotional intelligence. It is through this type of writing that many people are able to become comfortable with who they are, and better yet, they are able to learn exactly who it is that they are.

Tip 8: Walking Away

There are some situations in life that simply can be of no use to a person, meaning he or she should walk away from them. Such situations oftentimes include abusive relationships and/or the abuse of drugs and/or alcohol. Walking away from these things will help a person to become more emotionally intelligent because he or she will be able to think more clearly; thus, allowing the person to make choices that better his or her life.

Tip 9: Look for Strong Relationships

Strong relationships don't just come about in one's life. Instead, they are built. While it may not be the best idea to build strong relationships with a large number of people, it is important to build at least two or three. In doing this, a person will improve his or her level of emotional intelligence because he or she will be provided many opportunities to be empathetic towards those he or she cares about.

Chapter 3- How to Apply Emotional Intelligence Techniques to the Workplace

A group of individuals assembled to complete disjointed tasks for an undefined period of time must set aside some differences to achieve the goals. Leaders expect each team member to bring practical skills to the workplace along with an obscure ability called "emotional intelligence." In 1990s, psychologists studied the success levels of people with extremely high levels of intellect, which is measured through the intelligence quotient. Surprisingly, the people with average IQ scores reached higher plateaus of success than the geniuses. In addition, the average people had different qualities that had never been considered until emotional intelligence was outlined.

Most notably, these average individuals had the ability to recognize their emotional reactions to various situations and respond appropriately. The science of emotional intelligence has blossomed into a set of skills that can be defined, measured and developed. Applying emotional intelligence techniques to the workplace allows the individual to separate personal preferences from the tasks at hand. Mastering basic workplace skills can make all the difference in the pursuit of success.

Retain perspective – Daily frustrations can develop into actions that cause problems in the workplace. Other people deserve professional treatment even when personalities grate on nerves. Emotional intelligence at work includes the ability to overlook irritating attributes in other people to reach personal and professional goals. Challenging circumstances should be used to develop skills for the next opportunity. Perspective allows the individual to overlook the minor irritations that limit careers.

Develop workplace alliances – Accomplishing tasks requires cooperation between people at different organizational levels. From the first day, one of the highest priorities must be to develop alliances that will be helpful over time. Kindness is essential when learning the pathways through assignments. Peers, managers and administrative assistants play invaluable roles in the long-term success of the workplace. Access to the right people, supplies and opportunities can make all the difference in the years to come.

Check attitudes – Unexpected situations are common in most workplaces. Reaction to managerial decisions is one of the primary sources of angst for team members. Leaders play an important role in shaping the attitudes that develop when change causes discomfort and uncertainty. Each individual can demonstrate emotional literacy by applying careful thought to possible outcomes. Attitudes can exacerbate any situation if natural fears are allowed to run unchecked. Management of the situation can be less important than curbing attitudes that develop as a result.

Break emotional strongholds – In most cases, emotions arise from actions taken by others. Each person must stop and consider the entire situation before allowing an emotion to fester. Misunderstandings cause more hurt feelings in the workplace than actual events. Individuals who experience ongoing anger or resentment can enlist the help of an object third party to review the emotional reaction. Discussing the series of events provides a different perspective that can reduce the intensity of the response.

Learn to self-evaluate – Accepting blame for mistakes that were made is an important part of taking responsibility in the right situations. People who spend a great deal of the work week looking for someone to blame will discover opportunities are given to others. Performance evaluation begins with the individual. The ability to recognize areas for improvement provides a basis for helpful actions that cause personal and professional growth. Each year presents many chances to learn more and develop marketable skills. Emotional intelligence at work is demonstrated through the ability to measure, monitor, adjust and control.

Choose battles carefully – Peers discover which team members offer valuable skills and input for various aspects of each project. Trusted individuals work diligently and offer assistance when asked. Over time, the person who restrains his opinion will be asked for input more often than anyone else will. Correcting others is less important than completing the work and enjoying the journey.

Look for possibilities – Optimists devise solutions to problems before other people realize anything was wrong. Emotional intelligence includes the ability to listen to hunches that begin to tie symptoms together logically. Application of reasoning skills allows the mature individual to ignore the noise and devise workable solutions. Suggestions based on facts allow leaders to recognize the team members who are able to offer valuable solutions for the entire organization.

Mastery of skills that demonstrate emotional intelligence is essential for those seeking professional success. Progress can be made when one area is selected for improvement over the next 6 to 12 months. Attempts to incorporate every item on the list above will be overwhelming. Self-evaluation is an important precursor for the person who would benefit from developing higher emotional intelligence. Personal development is possible when the individual is willing to accept input from many sources, such as books, classes and other professionals. Priorities can be set according to the feedback received from peers and leaders in the workplace.

Chapter 4 - How Does Emotional Intelligence Help Leadership Skills

Some people study for years to become strong leaders, and others seem to be able to pick up the ability to act in a leadership role with ease. Understanding the best way to delegate responsibility and make necessary decisions for a business (or family) isn't something taught solely within the classroom. In addition, if a person isn't born with an innate ability to lead others, it's still possible to build such skills through an investigation of emotional intelligence, or "EQ."

The idea of emotional intelligence is easy to understand, but the concept does take some time to master. Emotional intelligence requires understanding one's own emotions while also being aware of the emotions of others. With such knowledge, a leader can make well-informed decisions that take a company in the right direction, inspire confidence in leadership, and allow a trusting environment to grow within the business.

The primary concepts of emotional intelligence include a self awareness of one's own emotions, the ability to regulate those feelings, knowledge of the feelings of others, and the ability to successfully interact with others with full emotional knowledge. Although the running of a business might seem like a very unfeeling and technical operation, managing emotional intelligence is vital for instilling confidence.

Understanding Self and Building Confidence

It doesn't matter whether someone shows his emotions outwardly or keeps them tucked away and out of public view because understanding those emotions is necessary for any type of personality. One of the benefits of understanding one's own emotions is that self-awareness makes it easier to recognize emotions in others and how those emotions might impact decision-making and opinions.

Once a person has been able to identify common emotional responses to various situations in his or her own life, an investigation of the potential strengths and weaknesses may commence. A leader must know for certain where he or she excels and where there is room for improvement so as to reduce the chance that employees or subordinates would feel less confident in that person as a leader.

Regulating One's Own Emotions

Knowledge of emotions isn't where building emotional intelligence stops. An individual must also know how to use and work with those feelings in any type of environment. A balance exists in being able to identify and work with emotions while also reducing the chance that those emotions would cause outbursts or bad decision making. Failing to understand emotions may lead to rash decisions where the outcome didn't benefit the company.

Simple knowledge of one's own emotions isn't all that is required of a good leader, however. A leader must also know how to employ those emotions smartly in any environment. This may mean practicing how to interact better with other people when a person is in a position of authority. Leadership isn't simply about ordering other people around. True leaders inspire people to believe that their way is the best way, and will lead to the greatest chance for company success.

Understanding the Emotions of Others

It is a delicate balance for a leader to be able to inspire confidence from the team while simultaneously creating a healthy environment where employees or team members may express their concerns or brainstorm ideas. Final decisions must come from the leader of the group, but subordinates often work best when they are able to feel that they have a positive impact on project outcomes.

To accomplish this goal, a true awareness of the emotions present in others is necessary. There are many common issues that impact teams that are easy to recognize for someone who has built his or her level of emotional intelligence. Failing to understand emotions in others means that a situation could get out of hand or lead to the destruction of the group dynamic. Understanding human emotions is a very fundamental part of human interaction, and it's a concept that good leaders will embrace.

Ignoring Emotions Doesn't Work

Paying no attention to emotional intelligence and attempting to lead a group within an emotionless void will weaken team confidence. Failure to consider emotions will also make it harder for a leader to solve issues that stem from an emotional connection to the work at hand; building a high degree of emotional intelligence in one's own self and allowing that knowledge to guide team decisions will create a firm leader from whom the team will gladly take direction.

Humans invariably make decisions based upon how they feel about a situation and today's most innovative companies and successful leaders all have a high degree of emotional intelligence. Issues of conflict resolution and building creativity during project building is a challenge for any leader to master, and there's no guarantee that what a leader tries will work. Emotionally intelligent leaders rely upon being able to investigate and implement a number of strategies to solve problems and guide teams.

Chapter 5- What Are the Key Points about Emotional Intelligence?

Why is it so important that we are able to comprehend psychological intelligence? Could there be several types of psychological intelligence? Is there a difference between women and men or between people who perform different types of jobs or between people in different age groups? Below are some of the key points you should know about emotional intelligence.

Emotional Intellect is Something That Can be Discovered as Well as Developed - Today, there are several ways to understand and educate people on psychological intellect.

Whatever your level of psychological intelligence, with the right help, dedication and positive actions, you have the ability to enhance it. Opposite of your intellectual intellect (IQ), which peaks about the age of 18 and stays continuous through the rest of your life until it begins to decrease with old age, your emotional and psychological intellect can continue to be developed and enhanced at any age.

Emotional Intelligence Can Increase With Lifestyle Experience – Psychological intellect can enhance as we age, it peaks in the 40s and then stages out. This might suggest that few new happenings will enhance our intellect after the age of 49. Research performed using the MEIR (Multifactor Emotional Intelligence Range) shows that psychological intellect does enhance with age, with major improvements between the younger puberty ages and beginning actual maturity.

Everyone Has Different Needs – We are constantly around different people in our families, groups or when we go places, and we are able to understand and use the right type of psychological material that is useful for all. However, some tasks might require different factors of the type of psychological intellect we use. For example, if your job involves a lot of getting in touch with others, you might need to be capable of handling feelings to help you cope with any storms. On the other hand, if you are a counselor, you need to be capable of comprehending your own feelings.

There are Variations Between Men and Women – In a research by Reuven Bar-On's which included 7,700 women and men, it was found that there was not a difference in men and women on the complete emotional quotient, but the women scored more on empathy, public responsibility and cultural connection. The men scored higher on assertiveness, stress control and problem-solving.

According to the study, women are generally more aware of their feelings, they show more concern, and they interact better personally and act with a bit more liability in public than men do. However, men have a better self-regard, they deal with stress better, they are more versatile, and they will fix problems better and seem more positive than women.

Showing Brilliance Adds to Your Common Intelligence – Whether you have a perfected method about buying your food at the grocery store, being organized and having your own strategic plan or life objectives, you must have an excellent IQ. When trying to fix a problem, being genuine about the possibilities does include a bit of know-how.

Not an Oxymoron 'Emotional Intelligence' – An oxymoron is a phrase that sends two opposite concepts (such as the word bittersweet). Emotional intelligence involves switching your feelings from the soft stuff to being methodical about your feelings and trying to understand things in a 'hard' way. We must have a nice mix of sensation and considering. Both are necessary to make the best choices.

Creating Decisions – Emotional intelligence affects our ability to create good decisions. We end up creating most of our choices based on our feelings, whether we admit it or not. Therefore, it is extremely useful in making good choices.

In Relationships – You probably notice more in relationships people with psychological intellect. They are the ones appreciating new connections. They are relaxed with who they are and being around others.

The actual term "emotional intelligence" means having the ability to identify, assess and control your emotions or controlling the emotions of others. This is born in some people, and others have to learn the process. You can successfully use emotional intelligence to get ahead in your life.

The key to emotional intelligence is hidden in four specific branches which are:

Perceiving Emotions
Reasoning with Emotions
Understanding Emotions
Managing Your Emotions

The ability to manage emotions is major when it relates to emotional intelligence. To get ahead in life, we must learn to practice controlling emotions.

Below are a few ways you can use your emotional intelligence properly.

Share your feelings with other people.
Learn how to tolerate others when they react.
Learn how to understand others feelings.
When facing a decision, think of all your options.
To fight your bad emotions, use the power of some positive thinking.

Using these tips above, you can learn how to get ahead in your own life by using your emotional intelligence. There is a positive result when putting these tips into action. The more often you practice these tips, the easier it will be for you to start using these techniques in your life.

Chapter 6- Developing Emotional Intelligence to Improve Your Mindset

Although just about everyone can give you a textbook definition of the work intelligence, it is a lot harder to define or quantify emotional intelligence. Some argue that it is something that you either have or don't have, but many researchers and psychologists believe that it can be learned. Also called EQ, emotional intelligence is the ability to understand and handle your emotions as well as reading the emotions of others.

Developing your emotional intelligence can allow you to become self-aware and improve your own mindset, and it can allow you to see the underlying emotions and motivations for others. Find out some of the key ways to develop emotional intelligence in order to improve your own mindset.

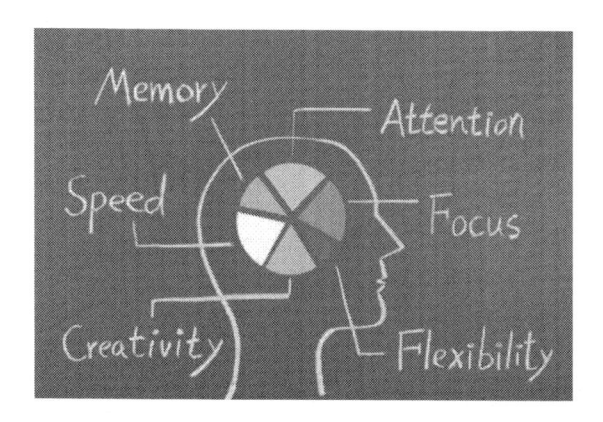

Understand the Importance of Your EQ

The first step in improving your mindset with a heightened emotional intelligence is to understand the importance of this EQ. For those who have a history of being stubborn or closed-minded, it can be tough to understand how this can benefit you in any real way. However, think back to the last time you were truly stressed. There is a good chance that you drank more than you were supposed to, slacked off at work or even said hurtful words to a loved one. If you could better understand your emotions and then channel that into something productive, your mindset would be more positive as a general rule.

Uncover Your Personal Stress Triggers

Stress is something different for everyone. Some people react when they encounter financial trouble, and others are stressed because of a demanding job. Whatever stresses you out the most; it is time to pinpoint the specific triggers. It's not enough to say that work, your spouse or your kids stress you out, because you need to be more specific. Examples of triggers could include:

Being late to work because of traffic
Last-minute homework assignments from your kids
A spouse who doesn't help around the house

Once you have your triggers specified, you can create a plan to avoid them. You might start leaving 10 minutes earlier for work each day, check homework assignment for the next day before dinner or create a housework plan for every member of the family.

Make an Effort to Have an Open Mind

A significant part of a high EQ is being able to understand all sides to a situation. Rather than feeling overwhelmed or angry by a specific turn of events, it is important to take a few seconds to spin it in a positive light. You may not truly believe it, but having an open mind is a proven way to think carefully about things and come to terms with them. Coming in for a last-minute shift on your day off might be annoying, but you can think about how someone else must be having an emergency and is worse off, or focus on how this means you get an extra day off from work in the future.

Aim to be Empathetic

A major cause of emotional distress for many is simply other people. Coworkers, acquaintances, family members and even friends can make you upset, but one of the key aspects of emotional intelligence is empathy. When others frustrate you, try to analyze why they might be engaging in the behavior that bothers you. When you realize that they are also stressed, tired, sick or angry, you'll gain empathy for their situation and focus less on your own perceived distress.

Be Reflective and Look Inward When Emotional

A lot of people who are under stress play the blame game which involves listing factors outside of themselves that could be responsible for the stress. When this happens, turn inward and focus instead on exactly why you are feeling specific emotions. Someone with a high emotional intelligence might realize that they snapped at a co-worker due to a looming work deadline, or they might uncover that the argument they had with their spouse was really due to insecurities because of a potential home foreclosure.

Identify Key Body Language Markers in Others

Along with identifying and analyzing your own emotions, emotional intelligence involves being more aware of others and their emotions. One of the most effective ways to do this is through body language. Being aware of how people move can reveal how they are really feeling and you can adjust your tone and language to help them be more receptive to you. Body positioning, smiles, stance and even how far they stand from you play a role and can reveal their inner feelings.

One way to improve your mindset is to fully develop your emotional intelligence, better known as your EQ. These tips can help you to do this, and the result will be a more positive outlook on life.

Chapter 7 - Understanding Emotional Intelligence and Communication Styles

Often referred to as "EQ" or "EI," emotional intelligence is defined as the way a person expresses his or her feelings, manages those emotions, and interacts with others who also have emotions. Sociologists and mental health professionals suggest that people who are successful in the workplace often possess advanced emotional intelligence. One of the interesting facets of emotional intelligence is that it's not a static number like an IQ. It is possible to improve emotional understanding and emotional intelligence over time.

Understanding emotional intelligence starts with an investigation of each of the central facets of emotional interaction, which includes four "branches" that cover all normal personal and social interactions in life. These different concepts include:

Emotional Awareness of Self and Others

It's necessary to identify the emotions impacting the self and to also recognize the emotions others are feeling. It's often necessary to figure out what type of emotion is being experienced before anything can be done about improving or changing those emotions. Moving away from negative emotions is almost impossible unless someone is willing to understand and investigate those emotions to identify them.

Thinking by Using Emotions

Using emotions to interact with others and solve problems represents a high degree of emotional awareness and the ability to use emotions to improve social interactions, work, and relationships.

Understanding What Emotions Mean

Emotions are often caused by incidents in life and it's vital to investigate how emotions spring out of events and also how emotions impact the decisions people make in regular social interactions. Understanding the cause of emotions helps a person to regulate their own emotions and also understand why a particular emotion might be impacting another person so strongly.

Managing Emotions

A full understanding of emotions takes a significant personal awareness and the ability to recognize emotional markers in others, and such understanding is often best accomplished by creating strategies to deal with emotions. Ensuring a positive outcome with the use of emotions represents a high degree of emotional intelligence.

A popular topic within psychiatric circles in the last century, the idea and concept of emotional intelligence received much attention upon the publication of several books on the subject throughout the 1990s. For individuals who aren't working in the mental health industry and aren't learning about emotional intelligence as part of a job, studying emotional intelligence has the potential to improve a person's life and make it possible to reverse negative emotions.

One of the primary benefits of a high degree of emotional intelligence is that the destructive feelings of stress may be reduced or even eliminated when a person knows how to recognize different triggers and the best way to relieve stress. Instead of allowing stress to consume a person's life, it's possible to reduce stress through mental exercises and avoid triggers that a person knows will increase stress.

Communication Styles and Emotions

The way in which a person communicates will impact how he or she is able to share emotions and understand the emotions of others. Sociologists suggest that there are four different types of communication styles. Figuring out a person's natural style of communication requires understanding each of these four types of communication approaches.

Conscientious

An individual who might be labeled conscientious will work very hard to ensure that they don't "rock the boat." This type of person wishes to stay within social norms and make sure that he or she fits into the accepted social niceties of the era.

Influential

A person exhibiting signs of an influential communication style will look to use communication as a way to convince others to believe something. Such an individual will operate very well in social circumstances and doesn't like it when the center of attention is elsewhere.

Steadfast

A person with a steady attitude will always look to see how they can fit in with their social dynamic and be an accepted part of a team. These people are willing to listen to figure out what they need to know and don't act hyper when they want something.

Dominant

As the label would suggest, a dominant person will look to create an environment that looks exactly the way he or she wants. Nothing will stand in the way of a dominant communicator who has a goal. Everything is a challenge to be overcome.

By figuring out a communication style, a person will be able to understand how he or she would naturally approach problem solving. When that individual is also aware of how to recognize common emotions, there is the opportunity to shape certain circumstances in such a way that there would be a positive result or answer.

Reasons Why Emotional Intelligence Is So Important

Improving emotional intelligence is valuable beyond the workplace, and even if someone is not employed in the traditional sense or is raising a family at home, being successful in life is closely tied to emotional development. Improvement in physical health, enhanced mental acuity, and better relationships are all possible with study of emotional intelligence.

Increasing emotional intelligence is a process that anyone may undertake, and it's essential to understand that such a characteristic is not fixed. With awareness of communication style, development of emotional intelligence may allow an individual to work better in groups at work and within the family unit at home. Continued evaluation of one's own personal emotional intelligence is vital as there is never a point at which a person is "done" investigating their social competence.

Chapter 8 - 7 Real Life Benefits of High Emotional Intelligence

Are you ready to learn the perks involved with high emotional intelligence? An increased ability to understand yourself and others has real world benefits, and will increase your success both personally and professionally.

Less Manipulation

An unfortunate fact of life is that some people view manipulation as a way to get ahead. Some common tactics include lying, passive aggressive behavior and playing martyr. People who have used these tactics for a long time tend to get very good at them; so good, in fact, that many of us find it difficult to know when we are being manipulated.

Emotional intelligence makes it easier to detect when a manipulative tactic is being used in a personal and professional environment. Responding to such a tactic in a calm and logical way usually deters its future use.

Increase Motivation

We all experience periods when we don't feel motivated. Increased emotional intelligence can decrease these periods. This is because people with high emotional intelligence know themselves better than those who struggle to understand why they feel the way they do.

Recognizing the real reason you are feeling unmotivated enables you to address the issue honestly. You will also have more self confidence because you trust your own thoughts and feelings. Being unmotivated to do your job because you're ill is not the same as feeling the same way because you simply can't stand to do it anymore.

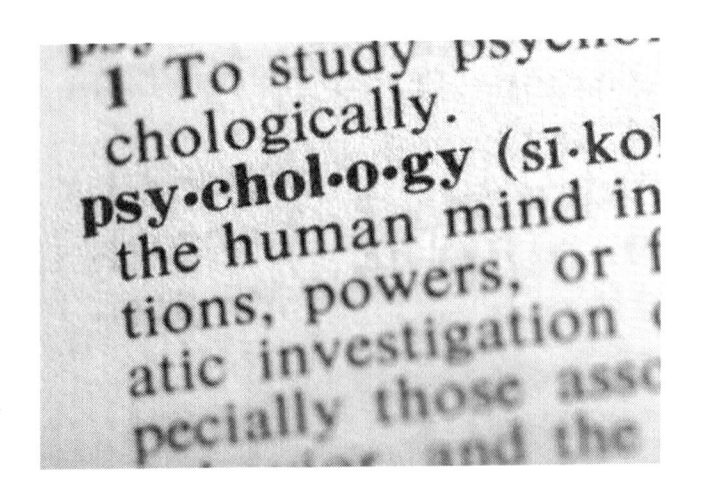

> 1 To study psycho-
> chologically.
> **psy·chol·o·gy** (sī·kol
> the human mind in
> tions, powers, or f
> atic investigation
> pecially those asso

Improve Difficult Relationships

Personal relationships improve with increased emotional intelligence. A noted difference can be seen in relationships that had previous difficulties. All relationships have ups and downs, and sometimes people get caught going over all the negative things that have happened. In a vicious cycle, this leads to increased difficulties in the future.

A person who increases their emotional intelligence, however, can break the cycle and improve the relationship. Instead of focusing on all the past hurt and angry interactions, emotional intelligence will lead a person to appreciate the positive aspects of the relationship and to respond in a more reasoned and less emotionally combative way.

Become a Better Supervisor

Supervisors who possess emotional intelligence are almost always better managers. They are able to assess work situations in a more logical way and not be influenced by emotion. This isn't to say that emotion is all bad; it's not. It's just in a work situation it is a better tactic to deal with employees, customers and vendors in a professional manner.

Managers with high emotional intelligence are better able to motivate their employees as well. Different employee types respond to different forms of motivation, and a manager with emotional intelligence will recognize this and act accordingly.

Emotional Control

Many people have at one time or another felt disrespected. This is especially true when dealing with the public. It can as an employee who works in a customer service job, or as a customer purchasing something from a store. When we feel as if we are being treated in a disrespectful manner, many of us respond by feeling hurt and angry. Acting on these feelings might offer momentary satisfaction but rarely leads to a successful interaction.

A person with high emotional intelligence can acknowledge how they feel and then choose the best course of action. For instance, confronting a sales clerk that you will never see again will probably make you feel angry long after the interaction is over. Choosing, instead, to simply smile and walk away will probably lead to you forgetting about the entire incident and being able to instead focus on positive things.

Wider Life Experience

Some people feel too anxious to try new things. Anxiety can lead to a lifestyle that doesn't allow the person to incorporate new experiences. This can prevent a person from doing everything from seeing a movie on their own to going back to school.

One of the most powerful benefits of high emotional intelligence is being able to recognize this anxiety for what it is and then working through it. Increasing emotional intelligence leads to a life that can be filled with rich experience.

Decrease Stress Levels

There's no doubt that life is stressful. The difference between being overwhelmed by stress and being able to deal with it often comes down to emotional intelligence.

Stress is often felt by folks who feel helpless to change things; emotional intelligence allows these same people to let go of these feelings of helplessness and instead move forward in life in a confident and healthy way. People who experience high levels of unremitting stress sometimes turn to alcohol, gambling or other addictive activities that only wind up causing more stress in both the short and long term. Increasing emotional intelligence is an excellent way to replace such harmful activities with helpful activities such as exercise, meditation and healthy eating habits.

About The Author

Terence A. Williams is a student of emotional intelligence and has pioneered the implementation of problem-solving skills. Employing emotional intelligence in business situations not only enhances the ability to empathize and pay attention to details, it also promotes the ability to focus on problem-solving skills. Some valuable problem-solving skills include brainstorming possibilities, negotiating through issues, offering comparative analyses, and examining both the advantages and disadvantages of particular situations in a thoughtful, engaging, and proactive way.

Terence A. Williams is big on allowing for creativity. Since emotional intelligence inherently involves a sense of creativity, those who endeavor the employ emotional intelligence into business situations must be able to demonstrate a willingness to allow and accept creative possibilities. In simpler terms, using creativity means being able to at least consider somewhat unconventional and unorthodox solutions to issues and problems.

What about reaching a compromise, Terence has mastered the art on the ultimate goals of emotional intelligence and in his book speaks about this in his book Is Emotional Intelligence Dead? Reaching a compromise without undermining or disrespecting the attitudes and value system of any one individual. In business situations, compromise can be a very effective way to resolve issues and promote overall continued prosperity.

Terence looks on these and other examples of some of the different types of emotional intelligence in his book Is Emotional Intelligence Dead?, that can be used in business situations represent only a few ways in which the use of such intelligence can create more meaningful communication, resulting in increased productivity as well as an overall increased sense of community spirit.

Made in the USA
Lexington, KY
30 March 2015